IN

M

LIVERPOOL HOME

All 163 Verses (and counting!)

Compiled and edited by
Gerry Jones and John Haines

Copyright information:

In My Liverpool Home

All 163 Verses

(and counting!)

Authors / Editors / Compilers:
Gerry Jones and John Haines

ISBN 978-0-244-09405-8

Published by Jones-Haines in 2018

For further information, contact Gerry Jones at:

gbjlcdb@gmail.com

Set in Palatino Linotype and Tahoma throughout

GERRY JONES AND JOHN HAINES

JOHN HAINES is a Seaforth based self-publisher of his own fictional works which he publishes under the name of Josh Rogan. He also republishes out of copyright classics. John is also an enthusiastic folk singer and musician and occasional song writer. In recent years he has formed a publishing partnership with Liverpool musician, historian and writer, Gerry Jones, with this very book being their second joint effort. John also collects first editions of the classics, is into gardening, but in a very modest way, basically – a single border. John also supports the great LFC. He is far nearer claiming his state pension these days than he is to coming of age. He is married with two grown-up children.

GERRY JONES is a resident of Liverpool, a long-retired teacher, and an active musician with an abiding interest in the City of Liverpool. Unlike his publishing partner, he does not (repeat, not) like football, beer, or sport. His main interests include: the "Liverpool Tart" confection, the "Lyverchino" coffee stencil, the Williamson Tunnels, folk-dancing clubs in Merseyside, European gatherings of folk-music and dance, as well as his CD, "Folk songs of Liverpool" – and of course the spin-off book of the same name, containing the words, music, chords, photos and information.

THE LIVER BIRD PIN BADGE

Our Liver Bird is seen in many guises round the city, with the Liver Buildings Birds taking pride of place. Just round the corner, by St Nicholas' church, there was a six-foot white bird on Mersey Court. Many other buildings and businesses use their own version of the Liver Bird as their "local" credentials. Small versions of the Bird are on sale including same small 3D free-standing "statues."

My favourite is the Liver Bird pin-badge, which, apart from being the cheapest, is most portable and visible, and I try to wear one all the time, either on jacket lapel, shirt collar, or as a tie-pin. I find it is great for starting conversations, even if only to explain that it does not represent a football club, but this remarkable city of ours. I also find it useful as a kind of "currency"; if someone helps me in some way, they will refuse "cash for a drink," but they will gladly accept my Liver Pin, and both of us feel that mutual thanks has been properly exchanged.

It can be found in some tourist outlets, priced at around £3.00 in 2018, but probably the easiest way to buy this badge is online at Liverpoolcitygifts.com in "silver" or "gold" – my favourite. You should be aware that there is a fixed postage charge whether for one bird or a dozen. To see their fine selection of Liverpool momentos, just go to:

http://www.liverpoolcitygifts.com/souvenirs?page=6

Finally, a warning; the pin itself is set below the centre of gravity, and so the Bird tends to "nose-dive". I am starting a rumour that if you let this happen, something unpleasant will happen to our fair city!

Gerry Jones – Liverpool – May 2018

HOW THIS ALL CAME ABOUT

By Gerry Jones

In 1991 Spencer Leigh of BBC Radio Merseyside devoted one whole session of his "On the Beat" programme to record his friends singing every verse they knew of "In My Liverpool Home". This became a BBC cassette containing 67 verses. Taken together, they make a unique history of our city, even an educational resource, so I tried transcribing this cassette, and this in turn inspired me to make them into a book.

There are still quite a few which are incomplete; they did not record well, or were hidden by the accompaniment; I am still searching for people who can fill any gaps. Then as years went by I realised that a lot of new verses had been written or discovered! These had to be added. No judgement; if they exist, they go in.

One problem I found was there are so many unknown people with "intellectual property" in these verses. But rather than lose for ever all these gems of our anthem (and their meanings), I have tried to find and credit each author, and I promise to give apologies and credit when an author becomes known. Thus, verses without names or initials alongside should be considered 'Anon', for now. For the following authors of verses, it was expedient to use just their initials, here are their full names along with their initials:

JH John Haines. GJ Gerry Jones. LcO Les Coe;
BBC = Anon, although gleaned from the Spencer Leigh broadcast.

CONTENTS PAGE

CONTENTS (CONTINUED) PAGE

NOTE; in some verses, **bold** or in CAPITALS are there to help indicate where the stress or beat should fall.

Some instances of ITALIC text mean something I am not sure about, usually a guess about missing words. Can you help??

Some items are **written in CHORUS format, so they are not really VERSES**. They have their value and their place in this book, but as they are not Verses, they are not numbered.

THE ORIGINAL SONG THAT GAVE US THE TUNE

"THE STRAWBERRY ROAN"

(First and last verse)

I was standin' 'round town, just a-spendin' my time,
nothin' else to spend, not even a dime,
when a feller steps up, and he says, "I suppose
You're a bronc' bustin' man by the looks of your clothes."
"You guessed me right, and a good one," I claim,
"do you happen to have any bad ones to tame?"
He says, "I've got one and a bad one to buck;
at throwin' bronc riders he's had lots of luck."

CHORUS:
Well, it's oh, that strawberry roan,
oh, that strawberry roan!
He says, "This old pony ain't never been rode,
and the boy that gets on him is sure to get throwed."
Oh, that strawberry roan!

I loses my stirrup and also my hat,
I starts pulling leather, I'm blind as a bat;
with a big forward jump he goes up on high;
leaves me sittin' on nothin' way up in the sky.
I turns over twice, and I comes back to earth;
I lights in a-cussin' the day of his birth;
I know there is ponies I'm unable to ride;
some are still living, they haven't all died.

CHORUS: Well, it's oh, that strawberry roan,
oh, that strawberry roan.
I'll bet all my money the man ain't alive,
that can stay with old Strawberry
when he makes his high-dive;
oh, that strawberry roan.

"In My Liverpool Home"

PETE McGOVERN'S ORIGINAL VERSES

1. I was born in Liverpool, down by the docks.
My religion was Catholic; occupation – hard knocks.
At stealing from lorries I was adept,
and under old overcoats each night I slept.

2. Back in the Forties the world it went mad,
and Hitler he threw at us about all that he had.
When the smoke and the dust had all cleared from the air,
"Thank God," said my old man, "the Pier Head's still there."

3. When I grew up I met Bridget McCann;
she said, "You're not much, but I'm needing a man;
I want sixteen kids, and a house out in Speke."
Well, the flesh it was willing, but the spirit was weak.

4. We've got wide open spaces like Wavertree Park,
where it's unsafe by daylight and more so by dark.
We've got places of culture like Dingle and Speke,
where they play "tick" with hatchets
and fight with their feet.

5. We've got romantic places like the Cast Iron Shore,
where you can find someone else's back door.
We had John, we had George, Ringo and Paul,
the Liverpool Spinners, and the St George's Hall.

6. The Green and the Orange they battled for years.
They gave us some laughs and they gave us some tears.
But the Wacker don't want no spiritual rewards;
all he wants is a Green Card to get into Ford's.

V1. The original six verses, as composed by Pete McGovern, and unleashed upon an unsuspecting world in the "Wash-house" folk-club in 1962, in "Sampson and Barlow's" restaurant, 39 London Road.

V2. This refers to Hitler's attempt to destroy Liverpool - Britain's main Atlantic port – by intensive bombing in May 1941, the **"May Blitz."** Whole areas of the city were totally wiped out, and the stress brought many premature births. These children are still known as **"Blitz Babies",** even though they would now be well into pensionable age!

V3. Pete McGovern did in fact marry **Audrey McGann**. Liverpool, with its Catholic Irish traditions did have many large families. Speke was a "new town" in south Liverpool, built to move families from slum clearance areas, and give them decent homes. In those days this was indeed a great improvement.

V4. Liverpool has many good parks, and Wavertree Park is quite central and spacious. Officially **"Wavertree Playground",** it is often called "The Mystery," because of old problems about its ownership. The Dingle, an area of dense housing in south Liverpool, was long considered a dangerous area to live, a reputation which Speke grew to share as it developed.

V5. Otterspool, once a natural riverbank, was bounded with steel and stone – **The Cast-Iron Shore,** or ***"The Cazzie",*** as it is referred to locally, and was used as a town rubbish tip. There is now a recycling centre there, and pleasant promenades and gardens, mainly a legacy of the 1984 **Liverpool International Garden Festival**, re-invented on a smaller scale in 2012.

The Beatles were from South Liverpool.

The Spinners sang as The Liverpool Spinners to play in Detroit.

V6. Green represented the Catholic Irish from the south of Ireland, while Orange meant the Protestant Irish from Ulster. Ever since the Famine drove them to Liverpool, there was dissent and enmity. A "Green card" provided a job for life in the Ford factory in Halewood – instead of casual dock labour, offering half a day, maybe.

PETE McGOVERN'S LAMBANANA VERSES

by Peter McGovern in 1996

Supplied by Honora Evans in 2017

7. It's yellow and fat
with its tail in the sky.
That menacing bottom
scares each passer-by.
Though it's an example
of genetic-led art,
we'll lose the Pier head
if it happens to fart.

8. A further portrayal in this modern day,
of Dolly the sheep made from lambs DNA.
Tail like a banana, head like a bull.
Just unzip the back, then peel off the wool.

9. In her stately monument Queen Victoria stirred.
A message had come from a cheeky Liver Bird.
She turned round in horror, with an imperial frown,
"We are not amused; it doesn't look like John Brown."

10. With its dinosaur legs and banana smooth tail,
a nightmare for those rolling home full of ale.
Imagine the shock; the poor wretch on his knees.
"I'm signing the temperance pledge; no more DTs!"

11. Oh, the legend of Troy, the well known Wooden Horse;
concealed in the belly, an enemy force.
Could a swarm of Brazilians from the lamb's chest advance,
to kidnap Michael Owen; stop him going to France.?

12. But this is just
joking. I know for a fact,
we love the unusual;
it helps with the craic.
So move it to Goodison
and paint it royal blue.
Stuck in front
of the goalie,
no-one will get through.

V7. The original is indeed enormous, and flat yellow – hence its name, the **Superlambanana**. Since then it has appeared in many sizes and guises, and has become enormously popular, second only to the Liver Birds.

V8. It can't be surprising that seeing as half of the creature is of the ovine persuasion, that a verse concerning sheep DNA was eventually written, and by who else but the witty Pete McGovern.

V9. The Queen Victoria Monument in Derby Square does indeed feature a solemn Monarch, the only major construction in the immediate area which was not destroyed in the May Blitz of 1941. Sadly, the monument has had and still does have a considerable number of detractors, and during WW2 some were even disappointed that it had been overlooked by the Luftwaffe; sad, but true.

V10. "DTs" ? "delirium tremens"
= "The Shakes!"

VERSES ABOUT PETE McGOVERN

13. His birth was at the posh end of Great Howard Street,
his last name was McGovern and his first name was Pete.
His first little words made the midwife turn pale;
he said "Stow all the Dinnefords;
bring out the ale." *(BBC)*

14. McGovern's a sportsman; he told me himself.
The trophies he's won weigh down the shelf.
He's snookered John Parrot,
bowled out Botham at cricket,
but he gave it all up for a Kop Season Ticket. *(BBC)*

15. When McGovern crossed the Mersey
from our Holy Ground,
they reduced Wirral poll tax by two hundred pound.
Now he's pals with the Squire of the West Kirby Pack;
wearing a T-shirt saying "Bring Maggie Back." *(BBC)*

16. Now, when Peter the Great wrote this wonderful song,
everyone sang his praises; said "It won't be long,
until Peter's up there with the Beatles and Spinners."
He said, "No fear; I'll stay here with my Guinness". *(BBC)*

17. "This song isn't long," the McGovern once cried,
but we soon realised that the great man had LIED!
"The chorus is fine, and there's nothing too terse,
but the rest of this song is
much verse and much verse!" *(BBC)*

V13. Great Howard Street is a major road through the dockside area of north Liverpool, and so is Great Homer Street, ("Greaty"), near the original home of the legendary **"Paddy's Market"**, and Jimmy Baker the dentist in Great Mersey Street. **"Dinnefords Gripe Water"** was a staple diet for post-war babies.

V17. Much verse, indeed. It has never stopped growing from that day to this. So much so that Tony Davies of the Spinners was moved, some years ago, to call it "That Monster!"

(Special CHORUS);

In my Liverpool Home, on Radio Merseyside.
They fixed up a studio for us to share,
and we'll go on singing as long as we dare,
and verses and verses and verses and verses!
In my Liverpool Home.

PETE McGOVERN'S
"WORLD IN ONE CITY"

18. So many colours and so many creeds,
all of them people, all with the same needs.
We MUST work together, and, understand, please,
to play the piano needs the black and white keys.

19. West AFRican ballet, Jamaican steel bands;
Irish step-dancing, and choirs from all lands.
Fierce Chinese dragons crawl over the ground,
a riot of colour of music and sound.

20. Senior CITIzens are marching throughout Liverpool;
they're starting all over to go back to school,
to study computers and using the mouse,
and taking "A" Levels in "Classical Scouse."

21. Let's TALK to the children,
their fears and their hopes.
We've GOT the experience to show them the ropes.
And working together, then WE can be sure,
their future is bright, and it's also secure.

All of the above verses were written by Pete McGovern to help Liverpool's bid to be **European Capital of Culture 2008**. We won the title, and since then Liverpool has never looked back. It made such a difference, and still does.

Pete always celebrated Liverpool's racial and cultural diversity. We see this today with such events and celebrations as Africa Oyé, Chinese New Year, and a strongly celebrated Saint Patrick's Day, reaffirming Liverpool's strong links with Ireland. Pete McGovern knew all this very well.

PLAYING TICK

22. There's a place in dis city where the nits de wear clogs;
they've six million kids and ten million dogs.
De play "tick" with hatchets, and I'll tell you no lie;
a man is a coward if he's more than one eye. *(BBC)*

23. Way out in Kirkby, the kids they wear clogs,
there's eight million kids and there's ten million dogs.
They play "tick" with hatchets, I tell you no lie,
and they call you a "cissy" if you've more than one eye.
(BBC)

TICK; the Liverpool word for "Tag" or "Tiggy".

V22. The Liverpool-based folk group the Spinners added their fair share of verses, which became better known than many others thanks to the immense popularity of this group. This verse often changes to mention Bootle or Kirkby. Being outside Liverpool proper they were for a while considered parts of "Lancashire" which was famous for clog-dancing, and the claim here is that even the head-lice were country-folk and wore clogs too. Kirkby and Bootle long suffered from a reputation as "badlands" where violent behaviour was believed to be commonplace.

V22/23. As so often in folk music, variations turn up in songs; obviously the same verse, but which came first? Will we ever know?

The Spinners use of "de" in place of "the" shows the strong links with Ireland, whose language has no "th" sound. So, "They do do that there, don't they?" can indeed sound like "Dee doo doo dat dir, dohn't dee?", as it says in the song.

THE LIVER BIRDS

24. "Who made our Liver Birds?" people will ask.
A German wood-carver was given the task.
Now when we hear . . . the Liver Clock Bells,
then we remember CARL BERNARD BARTELS! *(GJ)*

25. Our Liverpool Ladies will HUG and kiss men,
but a TRUE virgin Lady you'll FIND now and then.
Our eighteen-foot Liver Birds perched up on high,
will FLAP their great wings every time one goes by. *(GJ)*

26. The Liver Bird stands way above us so high,
looking down proudly on us from the sky.
There she is – so big and so proud,
standing majestically, over the crowds. *(Jean Johnson)*

V24. In 1908 he won the competition, in 1911 his Birds were in place. In 1914, war! Sadly for Bartels, he was interned on the Isle of Man just because he was German, and then deported in 1918. He was wiped from our history until 2011 when he was proclaimed a Citizen of Honour, with a plaque in the Liver Building. The Liver Clock "bells" are actually electronic chime bars. (Sorry).

V25. That is a long-standing Liverpool legend. You may have better luck with this one in the Museum of Liverpool, on the wall beside the great North Window. While you are there, say a little word of thanks to **Carl Bernard Bartels**.

V26. They say the Bird by the river is the Hen Bird, looking to see the ships and sailor boys coming in. The Cock Bird looks over the city, to see if the pubs are open. If these birds fly away something dreadful will happen to the city.

THE LYVER BIRD STENCIL

For both the Liverpool Tart and Lyverchino Coffee

This CD sized disc has a cut-out for shaking chocolate powder onto a cappuccino, giving us a Liver Bird on our coffee. It can also be used in reverse, to provide a "twin bird" image, or even a triple!

However, this stencil has another use; to put a Liver Bird onto a Liverpool Tart. (For the recipe, see page 59). Shake fine biscuit crumb onto the dark surface of the tart, producing a light "biscuit" Bird which settles nicely on top of the surface.

These stencils may become available for purchase, but with the aid of a pair of small nail scissors and some thin plastic sheets, they can be made quite easily and quickly at home. This principle could work for any image, such as a Christmas Tree, a Lambanana or an Everton Tower. So give it a try, enjoy the results, and spread the word of this unique emblem of our wonderful city!

FOOTBALL AND MORE FOOTBALL

27. Over at Anfield the shirts they are red,
the players play football as though they were dead.
While over at Goodison the shirts they are blue,
and the football they play is fantastic to view. *(BBC)*

28. If it's football you're wanting, the team at the top,
is the team that they're singing about in the Kop.
This city has got two great teams it deserves;
Liverpool . . . First Team, and Liverpool Reserves. *(GJ)*

29. If the Towers that look down upon Wembley Way
had voices to speak, then I'm sure they would say,
"Those Scousers are hard-faced, and they've got a cheek.
You'd think it was Anfield; they're here every week." *(BBC)*

30. Then one black day we lost Kenny Dalglish;
we hadn't much hope and we just had to wish.
The front line was weak, the defence was a mess,
but now we're OK – we've got Graeme Souness. *(BBC)*

31. At least twice a year the Reds play the Blues,
it's a major disaster if your team should lose,
Go home, kick the cat, throw your meal in the bin.
When your mates call, the wife says,
"He says he's not in!" *(BBC)*

32. Now I must confess I wear Everton Blue,
but I hope Man United do brilliantly too,
cause if they win the league as some hope and pray,
the Kop would be silenced which would make my day! *(BBC)*

33. The Vikings have landed, all with fair hair.
The Czechs and the Poles and the Germans are there;
all carrying banners. It's not world War Three;
they want to watch Liverpool - but can't get TV. *(BBC)*

V27. This song has given rise to many "football" verses, but, unusually in footballing cities, there is very little hate involved, with some families containing supporters for both clubs. They tend to regard supporters of the other team as members of their same family – but who need to be pitied for their mental frailty in choosing the wrong team to support.

V28. Naturally, this football banter works both ways, and is usually taken in good spirit and with a quick response. In the Boer War in South Africa, there was a significant hill called the **Spion Kopje**; the mound on which fans stood in the early days reminded them of this place. It became known for singing and chants – the Kop Choir – with one apocryphal chant-leader known as "Malcolm Sargent."

V29. In the 1960s, Liverpool and Everton shared top billing in British football, and tended to win the F.A. Cup at Wembley in alternation. This remarkable feat is, I believe, still unsurpassed, and is deeply ingrained into the hearts of the fans even today. In those days it was said you could always tell a Liverpool fan from an Evertonian; the Liverpool fan's Scouse accent had a slight Cockney twang – through having to spend so much time at Wembley!

V30. On Friday February 22 1991, Liverpool fans, and indeed the whole footballing world, were shocked to hear that Liverpool legend and manager of the club at that time, Kenny Dalglish, had resigned his position and left the club. He was replaced by another Liverpool legend, Graham Souness.

V33. Many different nationalities (although mainly European), can indeed be seen (and heard) in the city centre and around both grounds on match-days. However, rather than lack of TV coverage being the reason, it is more to do with low-cost air travel in recent years allowing many European fans of both our clubs, to travel back and forth as easily as getting from Dingle to the Pier Head.

AND STILL MORE FOOTBALL

34. Owld fellers with beards, kids in short pants,
in clubs round the country you'll hear the Kop Chant;
"I'll tell me Ma", " You'll never walk alone",
and – Shhhh! y'know what?
– "My Liverpool home." *(BBC)*

35. The Reds and the Blues, they've battled for years ,
they gave us some laughs and they gave us some tears.
But the football's as sound as a pound. For a lark;
go and see Tranmere – at Prenton Park. *(BBC)*

36. Liverpool F.C. they have had some success,
from league cups a plenty, but wait for the best!
The Euro cup beckoned, were were out of our minds,
especially when we won it a record FIVE times. *(BBC)*

37. As well-as-two Cathedrals, we've two football teams
and the angels in heaven think they're both supreme.
Way back in the Sixties they used to look on,
'cos the Blues had Angel Gabriel,
and the Reds had St John. *(Kevin Bargen)*

38. "What's your religion?" A feller once said,
so I put on me wellies and kung fu'd his head.
"All right!" said this feller, "don't get into a nark!
Do you worship at Anfield, or Goodison Park?" *(BBC)*
(*seen on a T-shirt.)*

V34. Football support in Liverpool is very much a family affair, with children introduced to the team they were "born" to support by fathers and/or grandads. Singing has always been an essential part of supporting your team. "I'll tell me Ma when I get home; the boys won't leave the girls alone." This Belfast song has precious little to do with football, or Liverpool, but it does help indicate the wide repertoire of the Kop Choir.

V35. Tranmere Rovers' ground is in Prenton, a district of Birkenhead on the Wirral. The team is Merseyside's third professional football team. Sadly, they are not always given due respect, instead being the butt of jokes (although usually without any malice behind them), by fans of the big two.

V37. Ian St John was a very popular Liverpool player, whose name (in the Kop) was always pronounced Saint John; you wouldn't get away with "Sin-jen" at Anfield. St John was shouted out after the "Kop Clap" when he was playing.

(Clap: 1-2 1-2-3 1-2-3-4 SAINT JOHN!).

V38. Being supporter of a team was (and still is), widely considered at least as important as your religion, although, unlike Glasgow, the two clubs are not divided on religious lines.

And a special **FOOTBALL CHORUS** (from Jordo).

In my Liverpool Home, In my Liverpool Home.
We've won 18 titles, no one can compare.
Meet outside the Kop under Shankly's glare.
If you want a European Cup we've got FOUR to spare!
In my Liverpool Home.

AND MORE FOOTBALL STILL

39. Scousers – the S*n says – are just all the same;
always the victims; they're never to blame.
Well, tell that to people who just went to the game;
life, hope and futures, snuffed out like a flame.

(Bill Baker)

40. When colours collide next the grey Mersey tide,
all fans will be spared from injustice and snide.
The Blue and the Red will once again roam,
freely and proud in our Liverpool home.

(Trish Torbet)

41. After the match all the winners will sup;
they'll open the bottles and fill up the Cup.
There'll be a great prize for the fellers who scored,
and two extra pints from the Milk Marketing Board.

(BBC)

42. Here on Merseyside, there's two football teams,
one plays at Haigh Road, the other's Marine.
Coz I'm a plastic Scouser I'll join in the fame,
but then say I am from Southport
when they're handing out blame. *(JH)*

V39/40. In 2015, after 25 years of injustice, **the Hillsborough disaster** in Sheffield was still casting a long shadow. The full inquest continued in Warrington, and even now it is hard to find a newsagent who will sell the S*n. (It is now *always* spelled with the asterisk)

V41. Although you'd think this verse referred to the FA Cup, it was in fact referring to the League Cup, which often bears a sponsor's name, or something which links to them. In this case it was the Milk Cup, as the competition at that time (from 1982 to 1985), was sponsored by the Milk Marketing Board, hence the quips in the verse about pints of milk being given out as part of the prizes.

V42. Marine FC play in Crosby, an area where working-class and more affluent areas are often hard to separate. Neither of these areas are in Liverpool proper, and in local government they are officially in Sefton South, linked with Southport, (Sefton North), which does not like its link with Bootle).

This monument to the disaster at Hillsborough was made by Liverpool sculptor, **Tom Murphy**, and is totally accepted and loved by all concerned. It is located very centrally, by William Brown Street, St John's Gardens, and the Birkenhead Tunnel.

CHILDHOOD DAYS AND MEMORIES

43. On Monday, the teacher enquired of the class,
"How many of you went to last Sunday's Mass?"
and we sagging kids, playing on Seaforth Sands,
with unblushing faces would hold up our hands. *(BBC)*

44. We 'broke up at last and the school is now shut;
got lemonade powder an' the sarnies all cut.
Those jellyfish in Seaforth did worry me Mam;
we'd come home back late on the 12. o'clock tram. *(BBC)*

45. "Don't be a docker,"a Headmaster would plead,
"Your career's up in town, now we've taught you to read.
Wear a collar and tie, Cherry Blossom your shoes.
You can start like Bob Cratchit and end up like Scrooge".
(BBC)

46. When our dad was at work and me ma was with gran,
we had our own latch-key and made our own scran.
The folks were not shirkers, nor saw social workers;
cos' we weren't on the skids, just happy latchkey kids.
(JH/GJ)

47. To go round the world used to take eighty days.
Now its only hours, in this jet-engine age.
You can breakfast in Cairo, have dinner in Rome,
then a great big fish supper in your Liverpool Home. *(BBC)*

48. Run down the floating-bridge onto the pier.
Straight up the gang-plank, "Hey! I want to steer."
Here comes the "Royal Iris", we're heading to war!
Well, not really! It's our day out on Egremont shore.

V43. In Catholic Schools in the 1950s teachers were required to conduct a form of verbal Mass Register. Not always reliable.

V44. Seaforth Sands, as well as Crosby beach, was where most of Merseyside went for a day out at the beach at weekends and during school holidays. Although not as common now, jellyfish, many of which could give a nasty sting, were a constant nuisance to beach-lubbers and bathers. For some families, the day wasn't complete without coming straight off the beach and into the pub, hence the line about the late tram coming home.

Up until the late 1950s, Liverpool had slow electric tramcars as its primary public transport. Only after they were gone, were they nostalgically called the **"Green Goddesses"**. Until then they were simply called "leckies" (electrics), as opposed to the earlier horse-trams.

V45. Cherry Blossom was a famous brand of tinned shoe-polish of the time, but also it was indeed used as a verb like "hoovering".

V46. The original latchkey kids were the many British children, who, during the Second World War, would come home to an empty house: father away in one of the services, and mother at work. They would have to shift for themselves, at least for a few hours: cooking their own meals, sorting out washing, cleaning and homework, until Mum came home. A few years later on, more in line with the sentiments of the verse here, it applied to all kids in the same position, no world war but with both parents at work, and sadly with some families, in the pub.

V48. Many Wallasey ferryboats were named after flowers, until the Iris and the Daffodil took part in the rescue of British soldiers from **Zeebrugge.** In recognition of this King George V1 gave them their "Royal" prefix, left to succeeding boats. The "floating bridge", usually called the "floating roadway," was a set of linked caissons down which vehicles could drive right onto the landing stage. It eventually rotted beyond repair.

49. Every Sunday from the Pier Head, aboard the old ferry,
were Eddie and Maureen and her young lad, Terry.
New Brighton was the place that we all thought was cool,
where a one-legged man dived right into the pool. *(JH)*

50. Coppers the enemy, the Teachers a pain.
Never saw the Headmaster until I got caned.
The Nit-Nurse a nuisance, but we knew the score;
just like me dad's belt, they gave us what for. *(BBC)*

51. Well I remember the best time I had;
we lived in a prefab when I was a lad.
In a little white cabin much joy could be found.
We thought it was Butlins – all the year round. *(BBC)*

52. The holiday season has come round again,
seeking a sun tan from Scarborough not Spain.
Your camera, your cozzies, your sunglasses packed;
and your wellies, umbrellas, and big plastic macs. *(BBC)*

V49. Today the only ferry terminals are **Liverpool Pier Head**, **Woodside** in Birkenhead and **Seacombe** in Wallasey. There were at one stage two others in Wallasey alone; Egremont Ferry was ruined during the war, but the New Brighton Ferry was very successful until the 1960s, when the piers at New Brighton became unsafe and beyond repair. The one-legged diver from New Brighton Pier was a genuine and well-known local attraction, with his cry, **"Don't forget the diver!"**

V50. The school inspections by "Nitty Nora, the biddy explorer," were always a worry, as the lotion to be used was considered quite smelly, and the name-calling afterwards hurtful.

V51. After the war a lot of essential housing was provided quickly by using identical plans and **pre-fabricated** sections. They were not wonderful, not meant to last long, but they were better than many of the dwellings which had been bombed. Many people have fond memories of their time, and for some it was a long time, of living in **"prefabs".**

V52. The British weather has not changed much, but this verse celebrates how things were holiday wise, before package holidays and cheap flights to the Spanish costas.

LANDMARKS

53. Next to the Black-E
stands proudly and high
a smart Chinese Arch
made for us in Shanghai.
If you Want your New
Year to be full of great joy,
say to the Lucky Man,
"Kung hei fat choi!" (GJ)

54. The Dockers' Umbrella has bitten the dust.
You might buy a Meccano, no charge for the rust.
Scottie Road is a legend now passed away,
but you can go down to Yatesy's and drink all the day.

55. Walton Gaol is the place for a quiet week-end;
climb over the wall, and you'll meet all your friends.
You can sit and watch telly, drink whisky and beer,
and chalk on the prison walls "Kilroy was here".

V53. In mid-February each year our Chinese community, in the oldest China-Town in Europe, celebrate a fire-cracker and dragon-filled New Year, all round the Arch and nearby streets. The Lucky Man is always there, dressed in lucky red, ready to give out a little packet of luck – a couple of sweets – to some lucky children. The whole area is packed with Liverpool people, and the local Chinese supermarket sells out of Fortune Cookies.

V54. The Liverpool dockers often walked under the Overhead Railway rather than pay to ride, and still kept out of the rain.

"**Meccano**" was a Liverpool product, made in Binns Road, Old Swan. Invented by Frank **Hornby** (of model railway and **"Dinky"** cars fame). Scotland Road was synonymous with "the real Liverpool."

There are pubs called **Yates's "Wine Lodge"** all over the city centre, and were noted for selling Australian White wine in a glass called a "dock" which could be large or small.

V55. The original Walton Gaol in Hornby Rd, north Liverpool, was built for prisoners from the war with Napoleon, and has been mostly replaced by Altcourse in Fazakerly. Liverpool has always had a criminal element, most of whom would know some of the inmates.

LATE NIGHT ENCOUNTERS.

56. I took a walk along Lime Street one day,
I saw a "young lady" a-heading my way.
"Have you got the right time, love?", says I to the lass,
she said, "I've got the time, Jack – if you've got the cash!"
(BBC)

57. I was walking along Parly one Saturday night,
I saw a young man underneath the lamplight.
"Have you got the right time," he said sweetly to me.
I shot off down the street, shouting "20 past three!" *(JH)*

58. There's Boozers and Night Clubs, right across town;
you'll find one that suits you, if you look around.
The girls are like film stars, you'll love them to bits,
with long legs, and mini-skirts, 'n' lovely white t..eeth. *(Lco)*

59. The ladies of Liverpool down Lime St. they prey,
all of the evening and most of the day.
But the best of them all is our own Maggie May;
and she'd see to the boys in her own special way. *(Lco)*

V56. For many years Lime Street was considered the place to find a prostitute. It was said you could always tell one, because they each had an "ankle bracelet/chain" – a sure sign. Sometimes she asks for "brass," to rhyme with "lass". "Jack" can refer to "Jolly Jack Tar", the name for any AB sailor.

V57. Equal opportunity employment in Liverpool. "Parly" is short-hand for Upper Parliament Street, a major south Liverpool Street, which has even given rise to our local tongue-twister "I chased a pup up Upper Parly". The street starts at the dock road as Parliament Street, then goes up past the Anglican Cathedral to the top of Lodge Lane.

WILLIAMSON TUNNELS

60. In Edge Hill today, if you go underground,
Joe Williamson's tunnels still wait to be found.
We can't find the end but they really look grand,
so come with your shovels, and lend us a hand! *(GJ)*

61. Old Joseph Williamson had a great scheme,
of tunnels galore, that was his big dream.
Edge Hill where his house was built over some holes,
Paddington was emptied by lots of man-moles. *(SR)*

SETH REEDER, from French Club and Friends of WilliamsonTunnels: "When I was in Liverpool in 2015,The House Site and Paddington were being cleared."

V60. Joseph Williamson started out as an employee of a Liverpool tobacco firm and eventually owned the whole company. After marrying the daughter of his former boss, he eventually branched out on his own as a general merchant. As well as becoming very wealthy indeed he was also a generous yet secretive philanthropist. Instead of giving charity, he employed hundreds of men on construction jobs, particularly demobbed veterans of the Napoleonic Wars who would otherwise have been destitute. In his tunnels, they came in as unskilled labourers, but many left as skilled bricklayers or stonemasons.

V60/61. The remarkable and mysterious Williamson Tunnels are still being dug out, some were originally open air quarries. Volunteers are welcome to take part in this re-discovery. Most of it is pick, shovel and bucket work, but you will be part of something great. Looking at pictures can never prepare you for seeing the real thing.

THE BEATLES

62. It was round Mathew Street
the Beatles were born.
The beat, the excitement,
the music, the storm.
I'll show you the Cavern,
now pristine and neat;
no hassle, no sweat,
and no rats round yer feet. *(BBC)*

A little humorous licence is used in this verse, as the Beatles were formed a long time before they had ever heard of the Cavern, and they were certainly not "born" in the town centre! But as the famous venue played such a pivotal role in their rise to the toppermost of the poppermost, as John Lennon used to say, it's not surprising that such sentiments are aired, whether whimsically or as if they are true.

Mathew Street still exists, as does a replacement "Cavern Club". This is a genuine club; go in, (if there's room), have a drink, hear the music. There is also a "John Lennon Bar", a shopping arcade called "Cavern Walks", and the "Hard Days Night" Hotel, just around the corner."

The whole area is very popular with tourists, and is the heart of the annual "Mathew Street Festival" of pop music. At the heart of all this, driving it along, is The Beatles. Their roots, their music, their influence, live on in this city. A massive industry, and yet this is the only Beatles verse which has appeared.

THE BUTLERS

63. Mrs Butler's eldest had a terrible dream;
he was playing in goal for the Everton team.
He held every cross with some fingers and thumbs.
When he woke from the dream –
– he was holding his plums! *(BBC)*

64. My name is Joe Butler, but I hasten to add,
that contrary to rumours, I'm not Billy's Dad.
He's not me brother; nor are we twins;
we work for the city but not on the bins. *(BBC)*

V63. **Billy Butler** has been a popular broadcaster on BBC Radio Merseyside for as long as anyone can remember, and he does introduce himself as **"Mrs. Butler's Eldest".** His reputation was set in stone following an on-air game based on a vocal "one-armed bandit," where right answers gave a spin of the "fruit machine". Billy was often heard to advise a contestant to "Hold your plums!" A perfectly innocent remark.

V64. Joe Butler was a founder member of the "Hillsiders" country band, on bass guitar and vocals. He played from 1964 till 1993. Billy Butler tells us that Joe sadly passed away some years ago.

If you said you were "working for the council" people tended to assume you meant on the bins collection service. "Me da werks for der corpy / der council," etc, was synonymous with working on the bins; an attempt to avoid a perceived stigma.

THIS AND THAT 1.

65. The Romans eventually beat Boadicea down.
They made their way north and reached old Chester Town.
From Caesar: "No further ; we'll camp here fair and square,"
"Why's that then, Jules?", "Coz there's Scousers up there!"

66. The Norfolk Broads
they have nowt on our
town. Forget glades
and weirs, and soft
bracken so brown.
Just get in your barge,
look out at stunned
faces, as you chug
along the canal
which goes past the
Three Graces.

67. Elizabeth Christian,
but "Lizzie" to all,
no matter the rain
or the wind or snowfall,
would sell flowers and fruit
from her barrow in town;
a real lady Scouser
a queen with no crown.

68. In this city of warmth, and singin' and beer;
the Battle of the Atlantic was directed from 'ere.
How were we repaid for this pivotal role?
Fifty years of heartache, of strife and the dole.

69. When you can't pay your rent or your rates or your bills,
there's only one thing that will cure all your ills.
Just flit up to Crosby or Formby so neat,
then you'll be nice and snug up in debtors' retreat!

70. When the bulldozers came to knock down the old flats,
a protester remained, surrounded by rats.
And then "Back Buchanan Street" did the man loudly sing,
from the very top window of the famous Bullring.

71. The famed "dancing waters" at Christmas were grand,
In Lewis's Grotto, the best in the land.
And when we got home, we'd sit on the porch,
with our gift from Father Christmas –
a multi-coloured torch.

72. In the courtroom I said to my Mrs therein,
"We'll soon we'll be divorced an' I'll celebrate with gin".
Me Judy she says, "Me six numbers came up;"
I said 'Let's try again, Lass, me sweet buttercup'.

73. John Moores and his brother between them they brought,
jobs to our city, connected with sport;
and catalogues for clothes, and toasters and clogs.
Dad did the pools, while Ma ordered togs.

V65. Chester was indeed the furthest that the Romans penetrated into this area, pushing due north instead to Lancaster and Carlisle. Chester means a camp, although the Romans actually named the town Deva, after the River Dee that flows beautifully alongside its medieval walls.

V66. This canal is a new attraction at the Pier Head, perfectly done after years of planning. It looks really superb, and connects Leeds right through the Pier Head to the Royal Albert and Salthouse docks, where there are now usually quite a few narrowboats moored.

V67. Many barrow-boys, and girls of course, selling fruit and veg., have come and gone, but Lizzie Christian is the role model for them all. Her descendants are still continuing her work and keeping her image in Cases Street ("Casey Street"). So many suffered the fate of those described in the "Barrer-Boy" song.

V68. Another remarkable tourist attraction in Liverpool is the **Top Secret Headquarters** in a Rumford Street basement, from which the Battle of the Atlantic, the convoys and the U-boat war was directed. This Top Secret place is now open for all to visit.

V70. The Bullring was the nickname of a circular tenement block – Gerrard Gardens – which was very popular when it first opened.
The **"Back Buchanan Street"** song – "Don't want to go to Kirkby" reminds us how many people still liked the place even when in later years it became a symbol of urban decay.

V71. Visits to a Christmas Grotto were a highlight of childhood, with many people still having fond memories of their favourites, usually Lewis's or Blackler's, now both long gone.

V72/73. New verses are still being written, as witness this reference to the National Lottery. Time was, everybody's dream was to win £75,000 on the Treble Chance pools run by **Littlewoods** and **Vernon's**. Both were Liverpool companies. Littlewoods Pools was originally owned by Merseyside entrepreneur John Moores, ably assisted by brother Cecil who ran the printing side of the business. But old John never stopped there, he also owned the Littlewoods and John Moores home shopping catalogues.

THE GRAND NATIONAL

74. At Aintree Racecourse, for many a year,
at the Grand National meeting, we all gave a cheer,
when an African prince, yelled 'I gotta horse!'
That horse is still running right on round the course. *(BBC)*

75. Get on your dad's shoulders and quick take a look.
The horses and jockeys go over the brook;
and then cross the Melling Road see them all come,
in front of them all is our favourite - Red Rum! *(BBC)*

The "brook", Becher's Brook, flows through the course.

V74. The "Prince" was a colourful Aintree tipster, a character who styled himself **"Prince Monolulu."** He did indeed shout 'I gotta horse!' but he died in 1965. No African Prince, he was born in what was then the DANISH West Indies!

STREET NAMES

75. From old L25 right back down to Kirkdale,
in our very own language misnomers are hailed.
"Anyone Westminister, or Parthenian Drive?"
God bless all Scouse cabbies who keep Scouse alive. *(JH)*

V75. Street names are pronounced the same everywhere? Once again Liverpool is different. Apart from Gateacre district, which we all pronounce properly as "Gattaker," some northern streets have acquired pronunciations which are widely accepted and considered proper. **Westminster** Road and **Parthenon** Drive and **Roxburgh** Street ("Rox-Berg") are some which suffer.

THE SPINNERS

76. If you walk down
James Street there's a
pub on the right;
not much to look at until
you're inside.
Just look at the walls as
you sit on your stool –
at the fighting ship
pictures all named
"Liverpool".
(Hughie Jones)

77. The Spinners sang folk-songs
for thirty-five years,
of shanties and clipper-ships,
of princes and peers.
They're known the world over,
but one thing still hurts –
the shock when I saw them in
those bright yellow shirts.
(BBC)

V76. This verse is from ex-Spinner Hughie Jones, and he sang it in **St. Nicholas' Church** – "The Sailors' Church" – on the decommissioning of the last HMS *Liverpool.* The bar is indeed as described, chock-full of great HMS Liverpool memorabilia. There have been many ships with this proud name; the last HMS *Liverpool* was probably the best of the lot.

V77. This Spinners LP sleeve photo shows those iconic yellow shirts. They were eye-catching, to put it mildly.

THE LIVERPOOL POETS.
THE SCAFFOLD

78. Now McGough, Patten and Henri are three of the best;
their poetry book sales still thrash all of the rest.
***The Mersey Sound*'s sold a cool million and rising;**
Well, they are from the 'Pool, so that's hardly surprising!

79. But this isn't all from the venerable McGough,
one group didn't cut it, it wasn't enough.
While the Poets still numbered this Litherland scribe;
he then joined the "Scaffold", a more musical tribe.

80. So along with young Roger was Macca's brother Mike;
McGear or McCartney, whichever you like.
John Gorman the last of the band that makes you think;
of the old Aintree Iron, or Lily the Pink.

V78. **Roger McGough, Brian Patten** and **Adrian Henri** were a co-operative of writers, specialising in poetry; they were at their height at the same time as the endless wave of local pop groups. Although Adrian Henri is mentioned in the verse as if he's still with us, he sadly passed away in 2000. Their book is still available in original form, and also in a modern version. A quick google on the title will easily lead you to the book.

V80. The Scaffold were an unlikely pop group, specialising in fun, comic songs, their most famous ones being *Thank U very much* (*for the Aintree Iron* - never identified) and exhorting people to *Drink a Drink to Lily the Pink* (Lydia Pinkham?) and her Medicinal Compound with its strange results.

SIR KENNETH DODD, (DODDY!)

Comedian – Singer – Actor

**81. When Doddy's on stage, there is nothing but laughter,
you're still roaring at one joke, then another straight after.
But your heart's fit to burst as he goes on so long,
the only respite's when he bursts into song.**

**82. Now Doddy is loved by all lower and higher,
apart from the caretaker who works at the Empire.
He's paid until Midnight, so come half past three,
gives the keys to a punter an' says 'Lock up for me.'** *(JH)*

**83. And Doddy, of course, has stayed true to his town;
and when the Royal Court was due to close down,
he said, 'Hang on there, fellas; let's stop now and think;'
and his campaign to save it put it back in the pink.** *(JH)*

**84. If a man wants a sex change, then we've just the thing;
he should go and see Doddy, our comedy king.
He'll laugh and he'll roar and he'll splutter and cough.
The man is so funny, he'll laugh his **** off!**

Sir Ken Dodd was a legend, unique and true to Liverpool. There really is a suburb called Knotty Ash; he did not make it up (although the Diddy-Men were his invention). Doddy started as a singer, and made some very successful records. He always lived in Knotty Ash, by Broad Green Hospital. And he was frequently directly helpful to local schools and hospitals. Unlike other superstars, he did not live in a mansion behind walls and gates, but rather, a modest house on a very public road. He died in March 2018.

V82. He could indeed run on for ages with a non-stop string of jokes, and his tendency to extend his live performances is legendary – but absolutely true. This verse may be an exaggeration, and the name of many other venues might have been used, but the basic premise is correct.

CHANCE ENCOUNTER

85. With Bessie on the Left Wing, and Doddy on the Right,
for years and years they did nothing but fight.
Despite such high tension, I just want to say,
they were both for old Liverpool, just in their own way. *(JH)*

86. Bessie Braddock, the lady who was in the last verse,
was a firebrand M.P. ; to the Tories a curse.
Woe betide anyone who took from our poor;
she'd stand up in Parliament and give 'em what for. *(JH)*

V85/86. Battling Bessie was pure Liverpool, a champion fighter for the poor and the under-privileged, with a heart as big as her frame. It is fitting that they both have a life-size statue in the main concourse of Lime Street station, almost facing each other. They were done as a pair, by Tom Murphy, and entitled ***CHANCE ENCOUNTER.***

LIVERPOOL CONNECTIONS

87. Robert Tressel, a writer, and builder by trade,
with poverty and death for his principles was paid.
He died in our city, on his way to the States;
the Ragged-Trousered Philanthropist
is now among mates. *(JH)*

88. The young Adolf Hitler once came to this city,
but caught Salmonella, at his digs, what a pity.
He never did forget the retching so bad,
so sent in the Luftwaffe the first chance that he had! *(JH)*

89. Hello, Holy Father! You've flown here from Rome,
to meet us and bless us right here in our home.
We'll wave and we'll shout, we're not going to stop;
a thousand times louder than even the Kop. *(BBC)*

90. While Hatton and Thatcher drew Handbags at Dawn,
along came two Bishops one bright sunny morn'.
The names of those clerics were Degsy and Dave;
they said "No more nonsense; this City we'll save. . ."
(JH)

Not every famous person past or present with local connections has a verse in this book, far, far from it. It simply means there are no verses that we are aware of that celebrate this actor's life, or that famous (or even infamous) institution, or this famous footballer, or singer, or politician, and so on and so on. It may be that some time in the future we may need to do a revised edition of this book, which would include other verses which have come our way. Then again – it may not be. Watch this space.

V87. Tressel wrote his famous book in 1910, and who died in Liverpool on his way to a new life in Canada. He was buried in a pauper's grave in Walton Cemetery.

V88. Adolf Hitler did indeed have family connections in south Liverpool, and it is claimed that he stayed in Toxteth with his **half-brother Aloys** some time in 1912 /1913.

V89. **Pope John-Paul II, Karel Woytila**, came to England once, and Liverpool was one of his venues. All the volunteer stewards lining his route wore yellow berets as the Pope-mobile went past.

V90. In the 1980s, Derek Hatton was Deputy Leader of Liverpool Council in the "Militant" era, when Liverpool reached its lowest ebb. Margaret Thatcher and her Conservative government hated the city.

Catholic Archbishop **Derek Worlock** and Anglican Bishop **David Shepherd** worked in complete unity to bring some peace and harmony, as well as healing long-standing religious divisions.

BBC RADIO MERSEYSIDE PRESENTERS

91. Alan Jackson has fled; yes, he's gone off the rails,
moved to the land where the cats have no tails.
He goes back and forth, winging over the foam.
If we only had kippers he'd have stayed here at home. *(BBC)*

92. All "On the Beat" but it's not C.I.D,
but a musical chat from our own Spencer Leigh.
He talks to the fans, plays music and song,
and he gathers his mates – to help him along. *(BBC)*

93. Author, announcer, playwright and wit,
a sound reminiscent of Guinness and grit.
young kids with the record, swing with his choice,
thinks Pavarotti from Scottie hasn't got a bad voice. *(BBC)*

This verse is about Brian Jacques (R.I.P.),
who was an absolute scouse legend.

94. Over the airwaves from near and from far,
come the sweet dulcet tones of Little William Maher.
He was called Little Willie because it was found
he could ride on their dog with both feet on the ground.
(BBC)

V91. Alan really was a sports presenter on BBC Radio Merseyside from 1980 after a career in the Isle of Man with Manx Radio. True-bred Manx cats are noted for having no tails, or maybe just a stump of one, so they may be known as Rumpies or Stumpies.

The crack about the kippers came about due to Alan's strong liking for the island which does of course produce its own famous and very tasty kippers. But, going by the sentiments of the verse, if Liverpool, or more pertinently the canteen at Radio Merseyside had a ready supply of Manx kippers, then, as the verse suggests, that may have been enough for him to stay at Merseyside permanently.

V92. In 1991, on BBC Radio Merseyside, Spencer Leigh devoted one of his programmes to "gather his mates", to sing one verse each of "In My Liverpool Home". The verses just kept flowing for a full hour, bringing the total up to 67, inspiring this book.

V93. Brian Jacques (R.I.P) was an absolute scouse legend. After many career changes including docker, seaman, cabbie and folk-singer, his main occupations were writing an immense amount of children's stories, and his Sunday radio show, featuring his wit, his rough voice, his accent you could cut stone with, and his encyclopedic knowledge of operatic tenors.

V94. "Little Billy Maher" as he is usually called, has for a long time been a popular presenter. He is also a musician, banjo-player, lyricist and recording artiste in his own right. For years he was a member of the Jackson's folk-group, and wrote many Liverpool songs.

(special CHORUS)

In my Liverpool Home, on Radio Merseyside,
they fixed up a studio for us to share,
and we'll go on singing as long as we dare,
and verses and verses and verses and verses..!
In my Liverpool Home. (BBC)

THE RIVER MERSEY

95. The Mersey it flows by our city so fair,
it borders the Wirral our neighbours 'over there'.
We have the great ferries and the tunnels as well;
our transport's not bad, but the travelling's hell!

(Lco)

96. The tugs on the river have plenty to do.
A rare breed of men in each closely knit crew.
They speak their own lingo unlike me and you,
and signal New Year with a "Cock -a-doodle-do!"
(*"Long – short – long – short – looooong!"*) *(GJ)*

97. When the coal boats of Garston went out from the shore,
they took all they could, and then a bit more.
When the wind and the tide knocked it over the side,
the Mud Men got free coal on every low tide. *(GJ)*

98. There's ships of all nations and flags of all lines,
crews of all colours, goods of all kinds.
Spanish and Russian and French, it is said.
Its a very small world at the old Pier Head. *(BBC)*

V97. In the days of coal-fired steamboats, the supply barges lost some coal, which was "salvaged" by local people, who were thus known as the "Mud Men of Garston".

V98. Russian was particularly heard further upstream at the Garston Docks, where the main trade was timber from Russia. The Russian sailors would welcome on board anyone (with vodka) who wanted to practise their Russian language skills.

CONCERNING CUNARD

99. Old Sam Cunard had the ships and the means,
to carry the emigrants, people with dreams.
They sailed from the Mersey their fortunes to find,
but me dad always said the best ones stayed behind. *(BBC)*

100. **(We) Went to the Pier Head in 2015,**
and who should turn up but the "Three Cunard Queens".
And after their journeys all over the foam,
we welcomed them back to THEIR Liverpool Home. *(GJ)*

101. Cunard had great liners way back in the day,
you could get on board if you had money to pay.
In May 2015 they were all back in line,
you could come here and see them
– if the trains were on time! *(SR)*

(Cunard's Three Queens visit coincided with a rail strike)

The Cunard Building is at the Pier Head, the central one of The Three Graces. The White Star Line building is behind it across the Strand – the "Streaky Bacon" building. The *Titanic* was built in Belfast, but Liverpool was her Port of Registry. There is a fine exhibition about her in the Liverpool Maritime Museum on the Royal Albert Dock.

SCOUSE HISTORY

102. Chuck in potatoes
and carrots and stuff,
cheap meat and onions
– just two is enough.
Boil in hot water
for as long as you wish.
Now you've made Scouse
– its our favourite dish! *(GJ)*

103. Some call it Hot-Pot
but we call it Scouse.
The smell of it simmering
sweeps right through the house.
You eat all you can and you sit down to rest;
if you open your shirt you'll find hairs on your chest.' *(Lco)*

104. Dockers had nicknames they used in The Pen.
Phil The Cot, and Drug Pedlar were hard-working men.
The Kitten, the Vicar and Nero all sang
of Little Red Riding Hood and the Broken Boomerang. *(GJ)*

105. The Tate and Lyle factory is gone from our town,
a poor dockside neighbourhood, that had "nothin' down".
But a beautiful village is now here to stay.
In Vauxhall we do things the "Eldonian Way" *(GJ)*

106. The demo men came to Montgomery House,
but they soon knew the building was made out of scouse.
The tower was rigged but the Dyno was dead;
I'm sure that Fred Dibnah
would have hanged his old head. *(JH)*

V102/103. Originally a stew brought by Norwegian seamen who called it **"Labskaus"**, it became known as "**lobby"** in North Wales, and "Scouse" in Liverpool. It was the dish of the poor people, who sometimes could not afford any meat at all, and this variant is still called **Blind Scouse.** Made regularly in many homes, it is now easily found in many places in Liverpool, including both cathedrals.

V104. There were so many dockers that learning their names and faces was a problem, but if you were told to find a certain man, he could be well-known by his appearance, his speech or his reputation. **Phil The Cot** had many children. **The Vicar** was a supervisor known for shouting " Ey! MEN!" **Nero** was always saying "fiddlin'" instead of the usual F word. **The Kitten** was always looking for his father; "Have you seen **MeOwld** feller?" **The Broken Boomerang** never returned from the pub after lunch. **Drug Pedlar** was noted for saying "Here's some **more for ya!**" **Red Riding Hood** – always went to his Granny's for lunch. **Dulux** always wore an ex-army greatcoat; "One coat covers everything"

V105. Tate and Lyle's sugar refinery, or factory as it's referred to in the verse, was a major employer and it was sad to see its derelict remains added even more depression. A keen group of local people based in **Our Lady's Eldon Street** pulled up the area by its own boot-straps and built in its place a delightful new village; canal-side dwellings, curving roads, lovely bungalow houses, and its own village hall, The McGann Centre, named for an inspirational leader.

V106. This demolition job on a Seaforth high-rise should have taken a few seconds, but due to repeated failures while trying to get the explosives to detonate, it took almost two weeks.

THIS AND THAT 2.

107. Young Bridget *(Cunard)* needs a good line in chat.
So I practised my lines on a dog and a cat.
"Can I buy you a rainbow, and the stars up above?
And in Sefton Park, we will make love.
Oh yes; we will make love." *(BBC)*

108. When you're on the last ferry,
but your works are a worry;
you've been on the Higson's, the pies and the curry.
And the toilets are broke and there's nowt else to do
make sure the wind's blowin', well away from you. *(JH)*

109. In Brookside's green Avenue Z-cars patrol.
Is somebody working while signing the dole?
Will Sinbad plead guilty – or is it his mate?
Oh, God! They're ALL at it – the whole damned estate! *(BBC)*

110. We get our traditions from our mams and our dads;
we live and we die as true Liverpool lads.
They all call us Scousers but we really don't mind.
We're proud of our city – we're one of a kind.

111. Amazed at the "Bolshoi" at the Empire one night,
was moved by "Blood Brothers" a Playhouse delight.
The Everyman's gear, but the honours must go;
rushed for me seat at "Ken Dodd's Royal Court Show".
(BBC)

112. Our May Horse Parade was a wonderful sight;
to get them all ready, we'd work through the night.
Hundreds of horses coming off vans and trains;
and screams from the muck-cart as the cleaner complains.
(BBC)

V107. "Oh, Yes, We will make love", was a popular song of the time, which has been neatly adapted here.

V108. Speaks for itself; Liverpool likes to Party, but that can bring its own problems. Higson's was a noted Liverpool Brewery for many years. Then Cain's flew the flag, with well respected beers – and owners, known as Sid and Bill. (Their real names had too many letters).

V109. Phil Redmond actually had a real Close of houses built as the set for his soap opera, and eventually sold off. The "Z-Cars" television police series was popular when Brookside started. "Sinbad" was the nick-name of a ne'er-do-well character, played by Michael Starke.

V110. "Scouser" is all too often used as an insult by people from other parts of the country. Probably from places which lack our sense of identity, and our pride in this unique world-famous city.

V111. There are quite a few theatres in Liverpool, of varying sizes. The Neptune re-opened in 2015, renamed The "Epstein" after the Beatles' manager. "Gear" is an adjective of strong approval or praise.

V112. Around the War period and even on into the late 1950s, most goods transport in Liverpool was by horse and cart, and a Monument to the Carters has been subscribed and erected in the Albert Dock village; a life-size model of a Cart-horse. (Not the much bigger shire horse).

VERSES FROM A 2015 COMPETITION

A competition was held in 2015, to discover what new verses had been composed, and no less than thirteen entries were received. Some authors were related to the organisers, so could not be allowed to compete. Some entries have been placed in other sections to which they relate.

The Winning Entry *(by popular vote)*, by *Tom Carter*

113. We've re-built our city, it's bright and it's clean.
There's New bars and restaurants, it's quite a chic scene.
The Arena has opened. Top bands come to play;
so get into Liverpool! You'll have a great day.

114. Scousers bring laughter, but they can make you cry.
They can lay you down low, then make you soar high;
playing their music and singing their songs,
about freedom and justice and righting of wrongs.

(Little Megs)

115. With Scouse-brows drawn on, and false lashes galore,
in P-Js and rollers, we visit the stores.
Our heels are worn high, and our hair-do's are wide;
on a night out we wear our Primarni with pride.

(Sharron Fidler celebrates the LIVERPOOL GIRLS)

116. Our Liverpool, our city, is one of a kind,
everyone's welcome, we're friendly, you'll find.
We're proud of our heritage; we know who we are.
We're scousers, and proud and the best by far.

(Carole Sanderson)

117. They say that the stuff in the Tate is called Art;
but me Liverpool mates say it hasn't no heart.
We saw those old bricks that had come from a 'ouse,
and knew that the artist had never et Scouse!

(Keith Dixon)

118. Well, this is my city, the place of my dreams.
A place where I've witnessed some memorable scenes
So come for a visit ; I'm sure you'll agree,
That the land of the Liver birds is THE place to be.

(Barry Robinson)

119. Now, Liverpool has changed, we got Liverpool One.
Fewer ships, fewer pubs and the dockers have gone.
But we still got pie an' chips, just to mention a few;
we can also have tea, and a buttered scone too.

(Bernie Jones)

120. If your wanting some bands then you need not look far;
there has been many a proper Scouse star.
From the Fabulous Beatles, to Cilla – our bird,
now known to all who have heard these great words. . .
"In my Liverpool Home. . ." *(Peter Ros)*

121. They say that in London if you drop down dead,
people ignore you and walk on ahead.
But here in this town, if you're starting to choke,
scousers will stop— and tell you a joke. . .

(Chris Muscatelli)

122. Ribble were the buses we rode into town.
The market was where the birds bought their posh gowns.
Yates's the place for your sorrows to drown;
if you missed the last train Shanks's ponies abound.

(Derek Torbet)

VERSES COMPOSED BY LIAM COLLISTER

123. Most people think that we's all "on the dole".
Think that we go robbing, taking what's not our own!
If they knew a true Scouser they'd know its all lies.
If they visited Liverpool, they'd get a surprise!

124. In our great town, we have had lots of fame;
some for good reasons, and others for shame.
We know the truth's out there; we always fight on,
till people stop thinking we's a ticking "time bomb"!

125. People in Liverpool don't care where your from,
they only know your somebody's daughter or son.
They'll take you in gladly, and give what you lack,
and then they'll confuse you by calling you "Whack"!

126. As Capital of Culture, we showed how its done;
we put on a show that won't be outdone.
There's plenty to do and a lot more to see.
The museums don't charge, so to get in is free!

The European Capital of Culture is a special status awarded to one or more cities within the European Union. It lasts for a full year, and during this time the city or cities who have been thus designated, stage a variety of events showcasing its culture and character. Such a designation can have financial and economic benefits and can see great regeneration occurring in the city. Liverpool won the title of **European Capital of Culture for 2008**, and we have never looked back. A panel of judges led by the late Tessa Jowell (RIP), MP and former Culture Minister, gave Liverpool the nod, edging out other cities who had been in the frame for the award: Birmingham, Bristol, Cardiff and Oxford. The decision was then passed on to senior judges in the EU for their final consideration. There were no last-minute hitches or objections, and the nomination was duly rubber-stamped. And what a year 2008 was!

127. Back in the 80's, the riots were mad,
and now people still think that all Scousers are bad.
Though people have labelled us robbers and thieves,
this isn't the truth, and its made us quite peeved!

128. With bands like "The Beatles", "Space" in the charts,
The "Kittens", one "Spice Girl", "Our Cilla's" a star!
"Frank went to Hollywood", the "Bunnymen" were gritty,
but "Gerry and the Pacemakers" - the sound of the city!

129. We've three universities within our great town,
and two grand Cathedrals that no one can crown.
We've fans who are Red, and we've fans that are Blue,
and will both join together to beat that Man U!

Liverpool John Moores University,
Liverpool Hope University and the
University of Liverpool, the original "red-brick" university

ELEANOR RIGBY

130. There's such a great statue from Old Tommy Steele,
it's Eleanor Rigby – the Legend, made real.
It cost "half a sixpence" – certainly a steal.
Some folks leave flowers to show how they feel.

(Dave Preece)

Tommy Steele did indeed provide us with this work of street art, in Sir Thomas Street. People sometimes leave a few little flowers, and spare a thought for **"all the lonely people"**. The song was inspired by a name on an actual grave in a Woolton churchyard.

INTERNATIONAL GARDEN FESTIVAL

131. Where once the big liners tied up to the quay,
dockside ....with its ....and its ....
We've re-built the Gardens, a Festival place;
a new start, a new Eden, a new Liverpool Face.

(Can anyone complete this verse?)

Back in 1984 the City of Liverpool had its great Garden Festival, achieved mainly by reclaiming some derelict ground. Sadly the main attractions became unprofitable beyond the festival itself, and became seriously neglected. Then in 2012 a serious re-build took place, although part of it was sold for housing, (with great views of Wales!)

THE LIVERPOOL TART (Edible)

132. For a Liverpool Tart take a lemon with zest.
For sweetening some Dark Muscovado is best.
A nice pastry base and a Liver Bird is neat.
The Liverpool Tart is our own local treat. *(GJ)*

LIVERPOOL TART recipe. Update.
Pastry; 8oz (200g), flour. 4oz (100g) butter or marg'.
1tsp. icing sugar. Pinch of sale. 4tbsp (20ml) cold water.
Line two four-yorkshire-pud greased baking trays.
Filling; 80Z (200g) Dark Muscovado sugar.
20z (50g) butter or marg', 1 egg, 1 lemon (unwaxed).
Melt the butter and sugar, then let it cool but not set.
Cut the lemon into pieces. Shred/blend till *fairly* fine.
Beat all items until *fairly* smooth, ladle into the pastry.
Bake at **Gas Five (375F, 190C)** for 17/20 minutes.
Topping; Lattice of pastry strips? Liver Bird shape?

INDEPENDENCE FOR LIVERPOOL!

133. Oh the world it is changing, it's altering fast;
................these mistakes, they emerged from the past
.... independence ... *(BBC)*

134. Let's follow the trend, and "Free Liverpool".
So raise up our flag over head the Town Hall.
Red and Blue stripes and a rampant football.
We'll have extra shops ....
and the Merseyside Customs ....close .... *(BBC)*

135. We'll base our economy on the export of Fun.
For defence we'll supply a new One o'clock Gun.
We'll tax all the imports, by road and by sea,
except, of course, Guinness, which comes in for free.

Please can somebody tell me what the words should be.
These three verses are part of one subject.

V135. At precisely 1.00 p.m. every day, until July 18th 1969, the Hotchkiss Gun on the sea wall at Birkenhead Docks entrance was fired by remote signal from its control box at Bidston Observatory, so all the Liverpool watch-makers could check their watchpiece timings.

PEARL ROYAL INSURANCE

136. Pearl Royal Insurance, a firm of renown,
have built their headquarters in the north end of town.
A fortress of steel, and sandstone décor,
to protect them if ever the PRU declares war. *(BBC)*

137. But nobody told them this important fact,
a large sandstone building will always attract
the neat housewives of Merseyside down by the docks,
cleaning their doorsteps with large sandstone blocks. *(BBC)*

V136.

The Pearl Royal Insurance company earned their place here by sponsoring the broadcast session and the BBC audio cassette which went on general sale after the event. Their Liverpool head office was housed in a very unusual "sandcastle" building, sited just behind the Liverpool waterfront. It does look as though it is built from giant blocks of sandstone, although it is indeed steel-framed. The PRU is the Prudential Insurance whose building was close by.

V137. Many older residents will remember their grandparents' generation taking great pride in having a spotless front door-step. This was done using "Donkey stones." (one well-known brand did indeed have an image of a donkey on it) which was used to scrub the step, down on your hands and knees, to leave a fine layer of fresh stone there, looking really smart.

SOME INCOMPLETE VERSES

Can you help fill the gaps? *(Italics are my guesses)*
Other incomplete verses are put by the subject they refer to.

138. Mam went to the pawnshop, ...
for now and again. *(it appeared)*..........................
..*(.there)* by himself.
(fighting *each other*?) for a place on the shelf. *(BBC)*

139. Feeding the pigeons down by the Pier Head.
..............for hours. .... overhead
Mama often told me, she swore it was true,
it meant some good luck if it landed on you. *(BBC)*

140. We've entertained Germany, Norway and France.
.... and traditional dance.
We've been to West Africa, Belgium and Spain.
Whenever we're homesick we sing this refrain... *(BBC)*

141. ....lads on the town.,
all on black velvet and drinking them down.
....no fuss.
It was down to the Pier Head to jump the last bus. *(BBC)*

Black Velvet was a popular drink at one time;
an unlikely mixture of Guinness and champagne.

142. The kids in the infants had*(sticky-bottle?)* lips.
Most sucked on a dummy until they were six.
.......definite grew, in their cheeks were impressed
and through the school railing they fed on the breast. *(BBC)*

143. We've lost Sturla's Pawn Shop
where Maggie May went,
it's not "Paddy's market" where money was spent,
it's not ....it's me.
... *(BBC)*

In the song, Maggie May tells us that overnight
she stole a sailor's clothes and put them in pawn.
She says it was *"Kelly's pawn-shop; Number 9"*

144. *(....................kind of brick floor?.)*
...........Leasowe Common ,
just off Moreton shore,
.... *(sheet?)*
and all of them free if
you're fast on your feet. *(BBC)*

145. It's sunny, it's lively,
the atmosphere's great,
but the pina colada .... till late.
The shows and the beaches
are really the gear
on the Costa del Moreton.
I wish you were here. *(BBC)*

146. .... started a pop group.,
...
Paul and George made it; you've heard them before,
but to lay down the key - was the REMO FOUR

V144/V145. Refers to Leasowe Common (near Moreton Cross) where this former light-house still stands. It was from here in the 1960s that the first-ever **Hovercraft Service** ran – from Wallasey to Rhyl.

THIS AND THAT 3.

These verses were sent to the editors quite recently. Several are by the same person, some are coincidentally similar. There is a main theme too: shopping and the High Street, but there's also the ever-present celebration of 'our' famous people.

147. With the old Green Shield stamps
you could get anything,
Irons, and toasters, and kettles that sing.
My Ma started collecting, she thought it was gear;
but the book's still not full, the shop's no longer here.

148. At TJs with Ma, I was always a-tizz,
as money went shooting right off with a whizz.
Packed in to small cylinders attached to a wire,
which shot off upstairs, going higher and higher.

149. Now some folks moan that there's too many shops;
but have they forgotten? We were once the very tops.
There was Blackler's and Lewis's, TJ's and C and A's.
And the tragedy of Hendersons going up in a blaze.

150. If you think that's the lot, then you are a fool.
What about the shop you got blazers for school?
George Henry Lees, yes, the one that was posh;
then off to BHS, or to Littlewoods for nosh. . .

151. My Ma went each week to the Coey for nosh;
she gave in a number, which made her feel posh.
She got Bacon for Pops, some biscuits for Livvy,
and got it all free, coz they paid out her divvy.

152. Most have forgotten, we had our own jeans,
a brand made in Walton, just perfect for teens.
To pay out for Levi's was purely for lemmings,
we'd nip off to Walton for a cool pair of Flemings.

153. Maurice Cole was from Seaforth, he was good for a joke.
He became Kenny Everett; found fame in the Smoke.
On the radio and telly, not a second did he waste;
and of course it was all done in the best possible taste!

154. Of poets and playwrights and authors there's choice;
between Russell and Bleasdale and Frank Cotterell Boyce.
There's old Beryl Bainbridge and Bread's Carla Lane,
Helen Forrester's the one for old memory lane.

155. If you're lonely, or sad, or feeling quite down;
there's one man who can lift any lonely, sad frown.
Ring up late at night, he'll sure set you straight;
Pete Price is his name, a Liverpool great.

156. The head of the Daleks at one time did groan,
and said to his minions 'Our chances are blown;
the new doctor's Tom Baker, a scouser so great;
he'll turn the tables on us!, shouting 'Exterminate!'

157. Anfield's the place fans watch Everton most
"Nah, that ain't right! Yer brain must be toast!"
"I assure you I'm right, and listen 'ere, mate!
I'm singin' this verse in 1888!"

158. When a wink and a smile does spell nothing but dread;
you know Anne Robinson's just messed with your head.
You'll get roasted on Watchdog, if you've sold the wrong sink;
you'll end up in tears if you go on the Weakest Link.

159. You could tell when the 'leccy man was just about due;
the kids by the meter would all form a queue.
He'd count all the pennies of which most he'd bag up,
what's left went to Ma, but soon she'd cough up.

Liverpool / Merseyside people love to reminisce about the shops we no longer have. It would seem that by virtue of their absence, they were better, and so it follows that the newer stores are often deemed to be not as good. What do you think?

Some verses celebrate some local worthies. Some of whom are well passed on, such as Dr Duncan from Victorian times. Kenny Everett (V153), whose most well known catchphrase after many of his outrageous sketches was 'It was all done in the best possible taste,' passed away in 1995. Pete Price is a good scouse with a great heart, and he is much loved for the great compassion (and sometimes tough love) he showed on his late-night phone ins for many years.

V147. Green Shield Stamps – a US idea originally: you buy something, you get a stamp, you save them up in a book, you redeem them for more goods. This was a national concern, but was much appreciated in the less affluent areas of the country, Merseyside included. It was popular and worked well for years, then business practises changed and the stamps were abandoned, and the Green Shield stores were rebranded as Argos.

V148. Many stores had this novel way of handling the customers' money. The assistant would place the cash in a cylinder attached to a taut wire, and then using a basic but highly effective form of propulsion, would send the cylinder to the cash room; very soon the cylinder would be back with the change.

V156. Tom Baker played a very flamboyant version of Doctor Who in the 70s and early 80s.

V157. Football now. Although most local football fans knows this, it is still a surprise to some fans when they learn that Everton, who were founded fourteen years before Liverpool in 1878, played at Anfield from 1884 to 1891, before moving to a brand new stadium in 1892 – Goodison Park.

V158. Anne Robinson is a Bootle born television presenter, although she started out her working life as a newspaper reporter. Her cheeky wink belies her tough character, something she used to great effect on the BBC quiz, 'The Weakest Link.'

V159. For many years, most people had payment meters for electricity. Coins would be fed into the meter to pay in advance for the power, but it was always more than the actual cost. When the person (the "leccy man") came to empty the meter, the kids in the house knew that (usually) some extra pocket money was coming their way from the rebate.

THE LAST VERSE

(Different Versions)

160. When the good Lord looks down, and to me he says,
"Sup your last Guinness; it's the end of your days".
I'll say to him that I don't want to roam –
I'd much rather stay in my Liverpool home.
(says Banjoman in Mudcat chat room)

161. Now, when I die no great funeral I crave.
No costly tombstone to put on my grave.
Just take me to [*Goodison*] and spread me around,
and they won't win a home match
while I'm haunting their ground!
(Phil Guest ex Mudcat)

162. OR . . .
When my LAST whistle blows & the "Ref Up There" says,
"You've supped your last Guinness, lad,
it's the end of your days."
Take my ashes to *(dramatic pause!)* Old Trafford!
(.. even bigger dramatic pause! Shock! Horror!),
and spread them around, *(pause!)*
and they won't win a match while I'm haunting the ground.
(Gerry's own preferred version)

Most singers end their "Liverpool Home" rendition with a traditional reference to their dying day, mostly about how they will still do damage to an opposing team from beyond the grave. This theme has resulted in quite a few variations. There is no "correct" version.

CHORUS-VERSES FROM ALFRED WYNNE

Alfred is an enthusiastic pensioner who came up with the novel idea of using the chorus melody instead.

As printed in the Liverpool Echo

These are not given Numbers, as they only fit the CHORUS and so are not true VERSES, but they are a "good read".

**In my Liverpool Home, yes, In My Liverpool Home;
the Handley, The Vaughan and the ferry, the tram;
the One o'Clock Gun and Red Rum as he ran;
the Saint George's Hall, and Paddy's Wigwam.
In My Liverpool Home,**

**In My Liverpool Home, never more will I roam;
our Tunnel of fame, and football, our game;
the Wellington Monument, Scottie Road and Green Lane;
Croxteth, The Dingle, Queens Drive and Park Lane.
In My Liverpool Home,**

**In My Liverpool Home, you are never alone;,
the Everton Toffee girls always around;
in Mathew Street there is a special sound,
when John Paul and Ringo and George are around.
In My Liverpool Home,**

**In My Liverpool Home, yes, In My Liverpool Home;
the Adelphi Hotel which I know very well;
the old Landing Stage with its wonderful smell;
the Seamen's' Orphanage where I spent a spell.
In My Liverpool Home,**

**In My Liverpool Home, yes, In My Liverpool Home;
the old Liver Building that makes me feel proud;
our very own accent that we speak aloud;
our Met' Cathedral where we're sometimes found.
In My Liverpool Home.**

IF YOU LIKED THIS, YOU MIGHT LIKE. . .

Gerry Jones' own CD: "Folk Songs of Liverpool" containing a goodly selection of these verses, along with 25 tracks of other Liverpool songs. Just Gerry and his trusty keyboard. Just email Gerry at gbjlcdb@gmail.com to order or enquire about prices. These are inclusive of postage and packing, and orders can posted out to Europe and worldwide as well as within the United Kingdom.

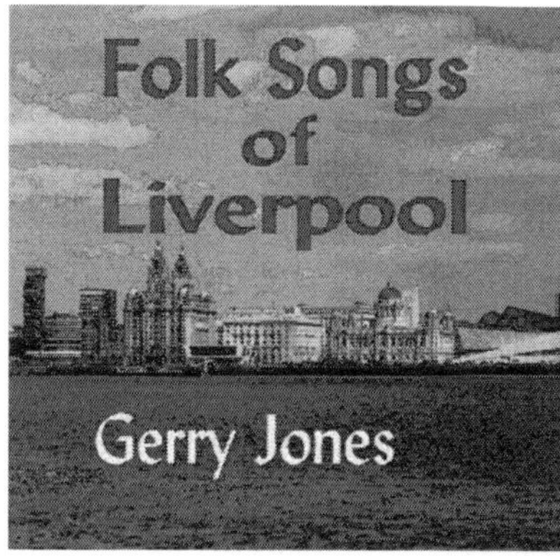

. . . Or – if you would like the actual music notation ("the dots") in melody line plus chord symbols, as well as the words of the other most famous songs, then the book, with the same title of "Folk Songs of Liverpool" is available for purchase from:

Waterstones, Liverpool One.

The Museum of Liverpool
at the Pier Head.

News from Nowhere.
Bold Street, Liverpool.

Pritchards, Moor Lane, Crosby

A print-on-demand version is available world-wide at Lulu.com and on most Amazon regions. Just go to:

http://www.lulu.com/content/paperback-book/folk-songs-of-liverpool/16252150

Or

https://www.amazon.co.uk/Songs-Liverpool-Gerry-Jones-Haines/dp/1326432419

ACKNOWLEDGEMENTS

Credit for starting the song in the first place will always redound to Peter McGovern.

Credit for the first collection of 67 verses must go to Spencer Leigh of BBC Radio Merseyside, who organised the radio session which resulted in the cassette.

OTHER VERSES as credited, and by "Anon" at BBC. I have asked around for some authors' names, but none have been offered.

PHOTOGRAPHS mostly taken by Gerry Jones.

Bio photo of Gerry; Stephen von Bargen.

Bio photo of John; Tom Niblock Photography

Photo of Pete McGovern; Liverpool Echo.

Ferry and River photos; Mersey Ferries.

Other images from free sources.

Before you go. . .

All the verses and the accompanying notes which you have just read are of course, all about Liverpool and Merseyside, its people and places. If you, dear reader, are not Liverpool born and bred, then don't despair. . .

Now, a big breath for your Mam. . .

163. If, for some reason – you weren't born round 'ere,
it's not a big problem – as long as you like beer;
and footy and music, and yer cat's a big mouser;
welcome to Liverpool, you honorary scouser!

And that brings the current tally of verses for this seemingly never-ending song to 163 verses.

Thank you for reading this book, and a warm scouse farewell from Gerry Jones and John Haines.

11293848R00040

Printed in Great Britain
by Amazon